FIRST NUMBERS

This book belongs to

_____

_____

GOLDEN BOOKS • NEW YORK
Western Publishing Company Inc., Racine, Wisconsin 53404

Golden Books and Design™, Golden Books®
and related trademarks and service marks are the property of
Western Publishing Company Inc.
Published in the U.K. by Western Publishing Company Inc.,
25-31 Tavistock Place, London WC1H 9SU

Devised and produced by The Templar Company plc,
Pippbrook Mill, London Road, Dorking, Surrey RH4 1JE

Written and designed by Mik Martin

Edited by Dugald Steer

Printed in Spain

ISBN 0-307-81481-5

FIRST NUMBERS

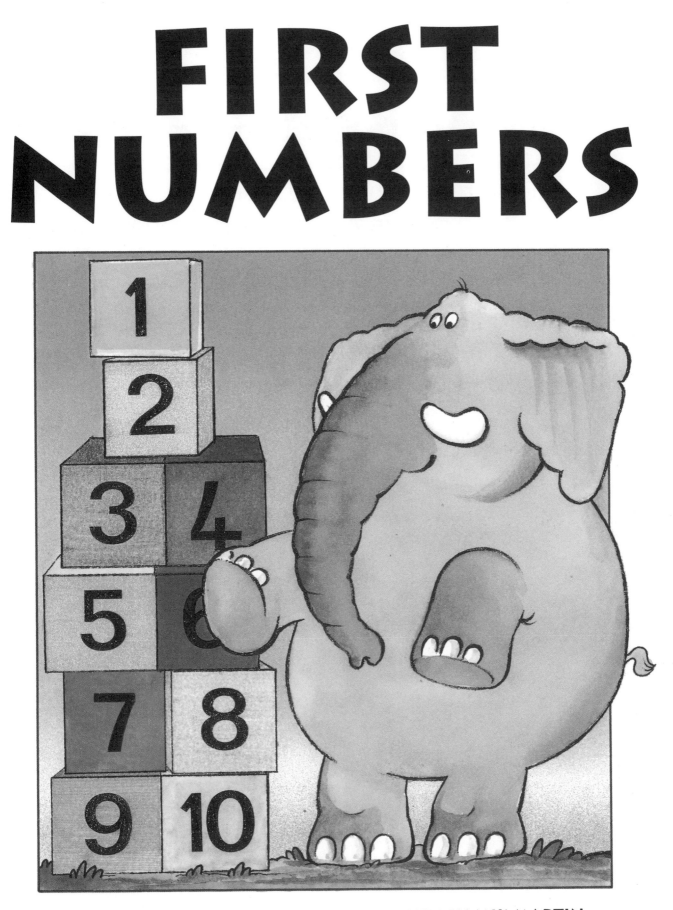

ILLUSTRATED BY JIM HODGSON • WRITTEN BY MIK MARTIN

Learning Land's First Numbers will help
get your child off to a good start.
Work through this book with your child,
explaining the exercises as you go.

Make sure there is a good supply of crayons,
coloured pencils and blank paper handy.
Soft coloured pencils are preferable to felt-tip
pens as the exercises can then be erased
for corrections or re-use.

Have fun!

Count the spots on each box. Say a number and then point to the right box.
How many boxes are there in all?

How many teddy bears can you see? How many ladders are there? Are there **3** owls?

1
one

Find the number **1**s on the fence and complete them. Start on the big dots.

Write the number **1**. Finish the line to the end.

2
two

These hungry cats want to catch the fish. Is there a fish each for them?

Colour the picture.

Write the number **2**. Finish the line to the end.

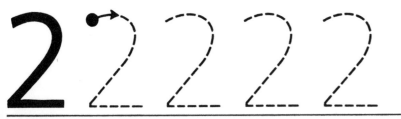

3 three

Draw a circle around sets of **3** things.

Colour in **3** of each.

Look carefully at the picture.

Find **2** butterflies

Find **3** flowers

Find **3** balls

Find **1** kite

Find **1** cloud

3 3 3 3 3

4
four

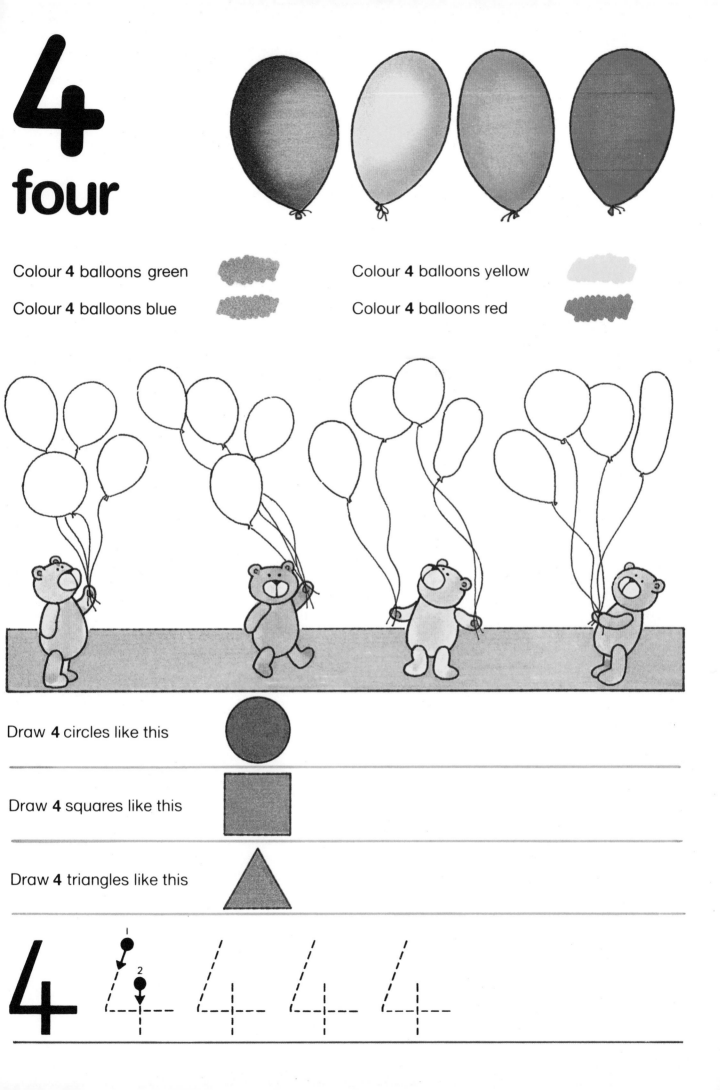

Colour **4** balloons green

Colour **4** balloons blue

Colour **4** balloons yellow

Colour **4** balloons red

Draw **4** circles like this

Draw **4** squares like this

Draw **4** triangles like this

Look at this picture. Write how many things there are in the boxes below.

Colour the buckets blue, the spades red and the umbrellas yellow.

How many buckets, spades and umbrellas are there?

Draw lines to the correct groups of objects. Colour the pictures.

Help the bears find the right jars of honey. Colour the jars the same as their shirts.

Fill in the numbers and colour the right number of objects.

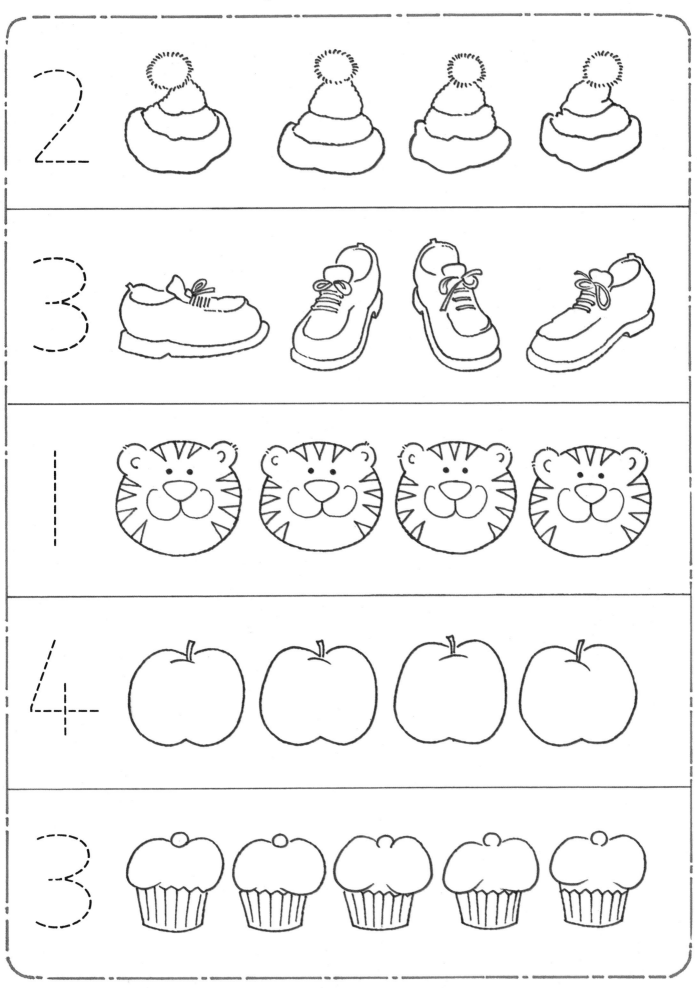

5
five

Join up the dots to make 5 objects each time. Colour them in.

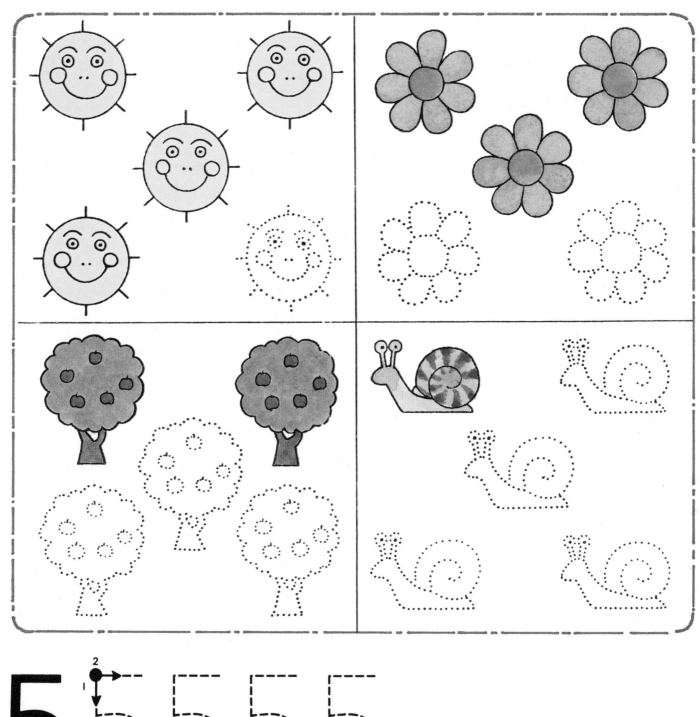

5 5 5 5 5

6
six

Diana Duck has found some food for her ducklings. To get home she must stop on each island in turn. Draw a line to show Diana's route.

6 6 6 6 6

Benny Bear and Tommy Tiger must catch **6** fish.

They can only see **1** fish. Can you find **5** more? Colour in all the fish.

123456 123456

Which boxes have the most in them? Mark them with a tick like this ✔

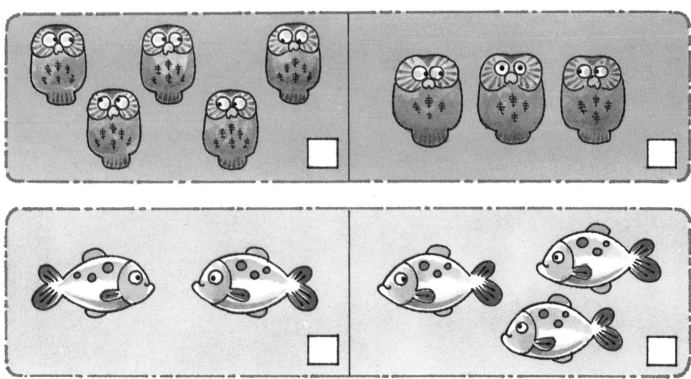

Which boxes have the least in them? Mark them with a cross like this ✘

Complete the missing numbers. Start at the big dots.

123456 123456

7
seven

Colour **7** stars yellow. Colour **4** blue. Colour **2** red. Colour **1** green.

Draw **2** more flowers to make **7**.
Colour them in.

How many objects are there?
Draw and colour more to make **7** each time.

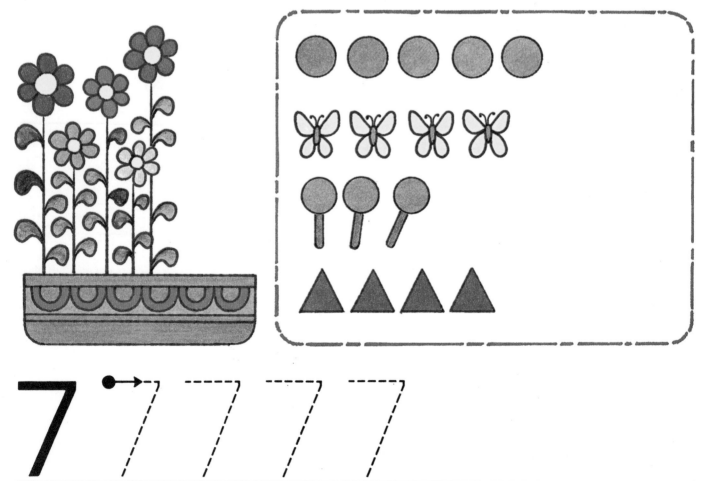

7 7 7 7 7 7 7

8
eight

Draw another cup to make **8**.

Write the numbers and join them to the right boxes.

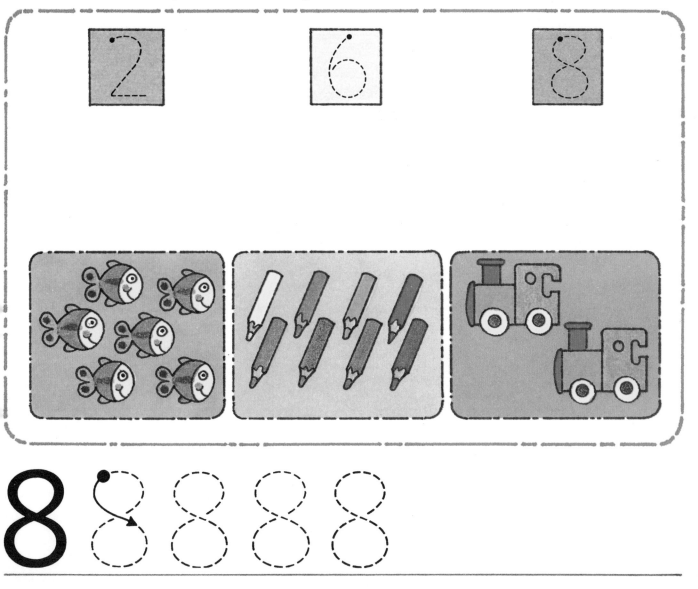

8 8 8 8 8

The animals are flying their kites. Colour their kites in different colours.

Write the numbers **1** to **8** below. Start at the big dots.

Write the kite number in each animal's box.

Now try without the dots. Can you remember where to start?

q
nine

Draw lines to join up the same number of animals or objects.

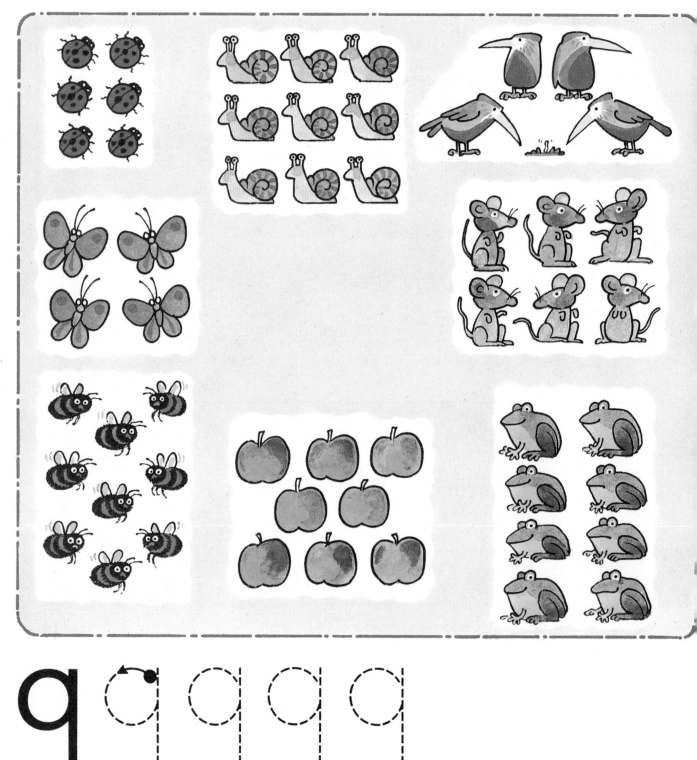

q q q q q

10
ten

Count the bananas. Are there enough bananas for all the monkeys in the picture?

How many bananas are left over?

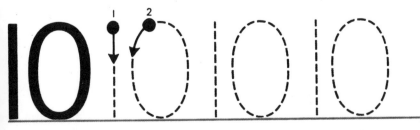

Join the balloons to the piles of presents. Colour them and write the numbers **1** to **10** below.

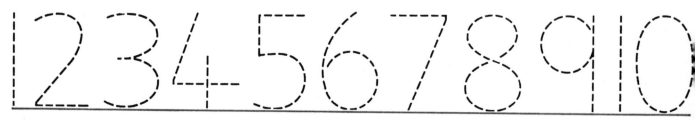

How many things are there in each box? Write the numbers in the small boxes.

Write the numbers **1** to **10** below.

Colour the picture using the colour code below.

1 2 3 4
5 6 7

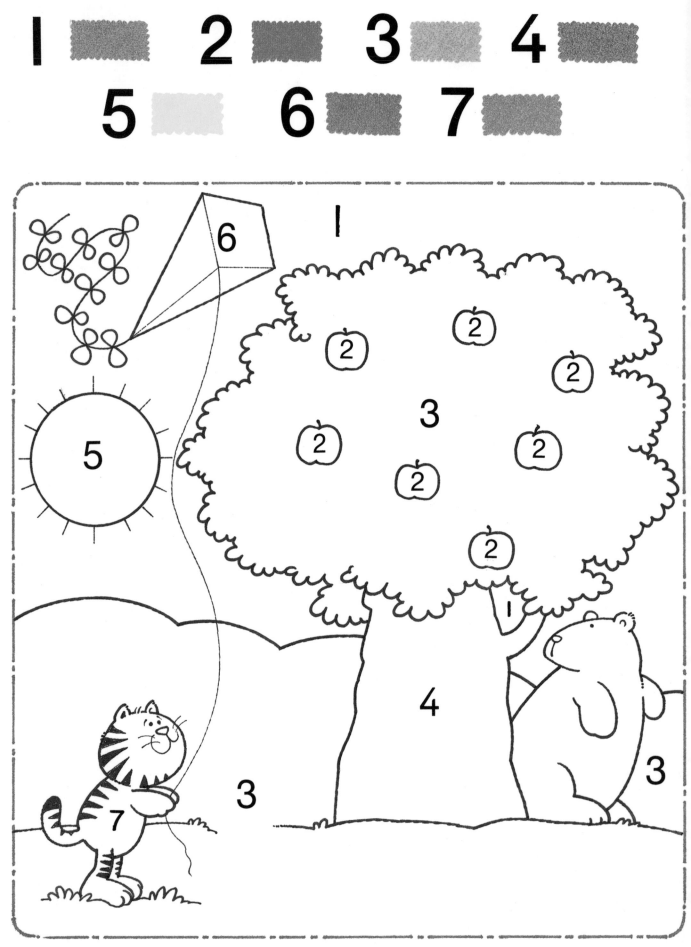

Who is hiding behind the tree? How many apples are there on the tree?

Complete the numbers. Count how many animals there are in each box. Put a tick like this ✔ if the numbers are right. Put a cross like this ✗ if they are wrong.

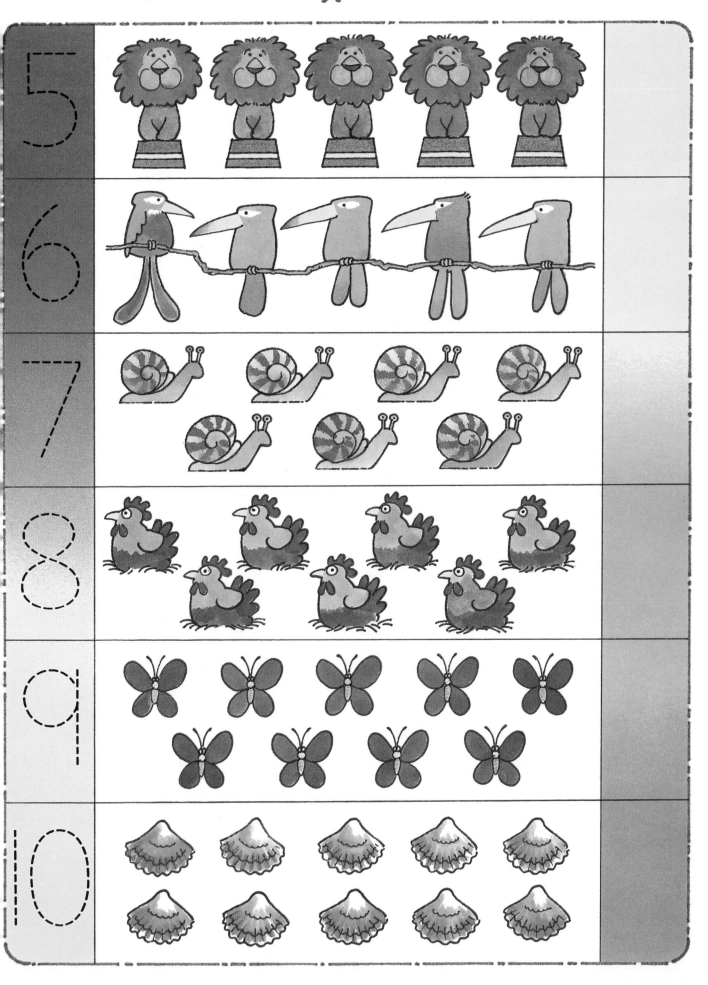

Complete the missing numbers.

Practise writing **1** to **10**. Colour the objects and write the numbers on the lines.

Here are the numbers **1** to **10**. Completely fill the lines to the end. Use a pencil.

1 1 _____

2 2 _____

3 3 _____

4 4 _____

5 5 _____

6 6 _____

7 7 _____

8 8 _____

9 9 _____

10 10 _____

Certificate of merit

This is to certify that

_____

has successfully completed

FIRST NUMBERS

Signed _____ *Date* _____

Use this **Learning Land** line guide for tracing on blank sheets or to photocopy.